STEAM MEMORIES: 1950's - 1960's
No. 76: SCRAPYARDS AROUND THE UK
DAVID DUNN

INTRODUCTION

The title of this album might seem a tad ambiguous when the locations of the images illustrated are examined and digested. Of the dozens which existed during the great cull of the last decade of BR steam, we present but a few - Cowlairs, Crewe, Darlington, Derby, Doncaster and Swindon represent the British Railways helping. To accompany them we have thrown in a few of the private yards; Birds at Long Marston, and Risca; Buttigiegs, and Cashmores in Newport; Hughes Bolckow, and Ellis Metals in the north-east of England. Added to the mix are a couple of images captured at Woodham Bros in the late Sixties when things were quite 'normal' and the storage area looked like any other steam graveyard – grim. However – you've guessed it – because we have shown simply a small selection of what is available for the series, we have enough illustrations and new locations to present another similar album at a future date. In the meantime enjoy this offering.

Thanks to The Armstrong Photographic Trust (ARPT) for the use of their material and also to friends Maurice Burns, Bob Lumley, Ian Spencer and David J Dippie.

David Dunn, Cramlington

(Cover) See page 71.

(Title page) Road to nowhere! BR 'Clan' No.72001 at BR Darlington's North Road scrapyard in October 1963. Maurice Burns.

Printed and bound by The Amadeus Press, Cleckheaton, West Yorkshire
First published in the United Kingdom by Book Law Publications, 382 Carlton Hill, Nottingham, NG4 1JA

Hughes Bolckows:

Having travelled from Scotland under tow, A4 No.60024 – one of four A4s dealt with at this yard – is a fairly new arrival in the Hughes Bolckow facility on 29th November 1966. *Ken Groundwater. (ARPT)*

6P and 7P 'Jubilees' and a 'Jinty' from the LMR add some variety to the place on 3rd January 1965. These are three of only seven London Midland engines which made it to North Blyth (page 57 of *North East Scrapyards* lists locomotives which were dealt with at Hughes Bolckow). *W.P.Hodgson. (ARPT)*

It didn't get much worse than this. Getting right into the yard now, alongside the quay where much of the cutting up was carried out, we get amongst the temporary inhabitants or what was left of them: The remains of B1 No.61167 and other locomotives 4th April 1965. Note that the windows are still intact. In the background, above the smokebox saddle, is the footbridge from where a number of the images latterly featured were captured on film. *Kevin Hudspith. (ARPT)*

Looking along the arrivals line – 29th November 1966 – with two A4s amongst the residents; In the background evidence of the ship building and repair activities which once played a part in the economy of north-east England. By 1966 everything was slowly being eroded by foreign competition, worsening domestic industrial relations, complacency, and social change. This view along the top of the boiler of No.60024 is interesting in showing a lot of minor detail and the 'bumpiness' of the Gresley A4 boiler cladding. *Ken Groundwater. (ARPT)*

Just to make sure they couldn't get away! No.60024 begins the indignity which will see it leaving the yard in numerous 16-ton mineral wagons. Note the Kingfisher crest plate still attached to the streamlining. The date is now 25th February 1967 and a start has been made. *A.Ives. (ARPT)*

Partly in the shade and totally disabled, BR Standard Class 2MT No.84011 is quite unrecognisable in this 17th December 1965 view on Battleship Wharf. *Kevin Hudspith. (ARPT)*

This is the first of three views of the Hughes Bolckow yard at North Blyth as seen from the aforementioned footbridge in August 1967. The coal sidings on the left served the staiths for which this particular port was famous. Bottom discharge hopper wagons dominate totally although in 1967 the seaborne coal trade was nowhere near as busy as it was pre-war. Panning round to the right to a point approximately half-way across the image we find the single arrival line for the scrap yard. We are now looking at private property where seven dead steam locomotives, including A4 No.60034, and redundant passenger rolling stock occupy one siding whilst 16-ton mineral wagons the other. The latter vehicles would be coming out of the yard in a couple of days, full with the parts of the cut up steam locomotives. A lot of the scrap would end up in various steel works throughout the country but some would go for export. The North Sea is out of sight to our left, as is the roundhouse of North Blyth locomotive shed. The place was a hive of activity – then – but time marched on: the coal industry was virtually 'wiped out' therefore, the staiths became redundant and, the railways serving the coal industry were likewise surplus to requirements, the scrapyard closed. A semblance of peace – where continuous hustle, bustle and noise had reigned for a hundred years or so – now broke out on this coastal patch. It is fairly tranquil nowadays but something important is missing! *Roy Stevens. (ARPT)*

The sheds in the distance form the premises of the business where valuable and re-saleable parts were stored. Just beyond, though not discernible is the quayside on the River Blyth; it was appropriately called 'Battleship Wharf'. Following that round to the right we can see piles of scrap on said quay, with cranes positioned in a seemingly equidistant manner; the cranes worked the main core of the yard which was the scrapping of maritime vessels. Not visible here but definitely in there somewhere was the public road which brought visitors to the yard in from the north. In the centre of the 'field' nearest the camera are numerous sections of Tyneside electric stock which have been put by for another day when things are quiet; note the two sidings which are located at right angles to the quay (page 58 of North East Scrapyards [No.19 in this series] has a panoramic view of the sidings in January 1965). They were empty on this date but at times they were full of carriage stock waiting to be dealt with; sometimes redundant corporation buses which had reached the end of their lives filled the field awaiting the chop – HB certainly enjoyed variety. *Roy Stevens. (ARPT)*

A further view of the Hughes Bolckow yard in August 1967! From the same bridge we are now looking virtually due west. This image reveals an ex-Royal Navy Destroyer, D15 H.M.S. Cavendish, which had recently been disposed of by the RN and had arrived at Blyth that very month. The fact that the mast had already been demolished shows that a start had been made on scrapping the ship shortly after arrival. A member of 'C' class – also known as 'Emergency War Design Destroyers' – the 2530-ton vessel was built by J.Brown & Co. at Clydebank and commissioned in January 1945, joining the Home Fleet and carrying out mainly escort duties. Shortly after VE day she left for the Far East but hostilities ended there before her arrival and she came back to the UK. Between 1946 and 1965 she served in almost equal measure between the Home Fleet, Mediterranean Fleet, Far East Fleet and Reserve Fleet. In 1965 she was taken in hand for modernisation at Portsmouth but it was never completed and she was put on the Disposal List in early 1967. The ships motto 'Safe by Taking Care' was way ahead of its time and could be construed to be part of an advert for condoms or perhaps a leader for a H&SE campaign! The only UK WW2 Destroyer surviving is HMS Cavalier D73 – a sister to D15 – which is preserved at the Chatham Historic Ships Site, the old Chatham Dockyard. This image especially reminds us that many of the yards where steam locomotives were scrapped during those dark days of the 1960s had other more reliable and long-standing elements on which to work. Across the river is Bates Colliery, recently modernised and good for another couple of decades – that was the plan anyway. *Roy Stevens. (ARPT)*

The view from the road looking east into the yard in August 1967! Appearing more like the aftermath of a tragic accident, the former Tyneside EMUs litter the premises. Inside the nearest car – E29236E – a scrapman goes about his task with only his bonus in mind. The prize here were the electric motors set into the bogies but quite a lot of debris would have to be cleared before they were accessible. *Roy Stevens. (ARPT)*

Before, and after views. Nothing could survive those curves! North Tyneside electric units at Hughes in 1966. *D.Dunn coll.*

A relatively tidy area of the yard: Looking north onto the quay where many of the steam locomotive met their fate, as did numerous sea-going vessels. The notice states: 'Warning – Beware of Rail Traffic Here'. The quadruple chimneys of Blyth power station own the background. *Malcolm Dunnett.*

This ships figurehead greeted visitors as they arrived at the Hughes Bolckow offices and works entrance. It is the restored original from H.M.S. Southampton, certainly the first Royal Navy ship which HB broke-up and possibly the first ship scrapped at the North Blyth quayside site. When the Hughes Bolckow premises closed the figurehead was rescued from outside the building but as it was being positioned onto a waiting road vehicle, it sadly fell apart. Whatever happened to it after that catastrophic event is unknown. *Malcolm Dunnett. (ARPT)*

15

Ellis Metals:

(this page and opposite) Ellis Metals at Swalwell, on the south bank of the River Tyne near Derwenthaugh, was an established yard looking after local requirements. It was connected to the rail network for despatching wagon loads of scrap to the appropriate works. The Company was another of the north-east England firms which suddenly started taking in condemned steam locomotives mainly from local depots. Although they scrapped less than thirty locomotives – and one of those was boiler-less – the yard managed half a dozen each of the V2 class, Q6, and WD 2-8-0, with others joining the mix including a couple of former LMS designs. Of the V2s, No.60865 and 60901 were photographed in the premises in the summer of 1965. Both were ex-Gateshead engines although the external condition of 60865 would have us believe otherwise. They had been condemned on the same day – 14th June – and sold to Ellis in July. *both Bob Lumley.*

Cashmore's Newport:

Cashmore's, Newport, Monmouthshire: 'West Country' No.34021 ex-DARTMOOR, about to undergo the transformation from organised metal to scrap! The date is 25th February 1968, a Sunday, and the only movement in the yard appears to be wandering enthusiasts who have made the journey to see for themselves that mountain of assorted locomotives parts. There were other non-railway items in there including a former armoured fighting vehicle – 'lot 11' take it away yourselves – apparently one of many. Cashmore's had another yard at Great Bridge in the heart of the Black Country and it was from that location where most of the scrap generated by the company was returned to the metal industry. Whereas Great Bridge dealt with locomotives mainly from the ER, LMR, and WR, the Newport yard had, by dint of its geographical location, an appetite for SR, WR and LM locomotives. *Norman Preedy.*

At the end of the previous October – 22nd, another Sunday – and the view of the yard from the same vantage point is only slightly different. The locomotive for instance is changed; this is BR Standard No.73022 with the boiler and firebox virtually removed! The scrap mountain appears to be unaltered but without detective-like methods of examination it would be difficult to be certain one way or the other. Did a certain scrapyard in Leicester get the inspiration to create an even bigger mountain of scrap after seeing this steam-age example I wonder? *Norman Preedy.*

(above) This was the queue outside Cashmore's on 26th March 1968 – an everyday scene during those few years when the yard gained a certain infamy amongst the railway fraternity. This line includes a pair of SR Pacifics, Nos.34087, 34018, and one of the USA 0-6-0T, No.30069. Note the BR Standard tender buffered up to 145 SQUADRON – on first glance, those tenders could have got away with being coupled to these Pacifics, at a pinch! *(below)* On Sunday 17th December 1967 the queue consisted of Nos.34013 OKEHAMPTON, 35003 ROYAL MAIL, and 34004 YEOVIL. both images *Norman Preedy.*

Two views of the Cashmore's queue on a rather dull and sombre Tuesday 23rd August 1966; again Southern Region engines dominate. Considering that the 'light' Pacific had only been withdrawn some six months previously, it appears to have suffered from some serious cannibalisation during that period. *K.Gregory. (ARPT)*

Buttigieg's, Newport:

British Oxygen supplied most of the gases used by industry and the amount of gas used by the UK scrapyards during the great cull of the 1960s must have given the profits a healthy appearance. The number of gas bottles, or cylinders, strewn around the yards and the nature in which they were 'stored' might have frightened off representatives from the company during that period of great industry but nowadays scenes such as this would not be tolerated by Government inspectors. Miraculously, accidents and fatalities concerning gas bottles were few, which is surprising when the potential for disaster was evident in virtually every yard throughout the land. This is Buttigieg's at Newport where SR Pacifics were also amongst the favourites, not to mention Stanier 8Fs and BR Standards. On show here on a much brighter Sunday 22nd October 1967, are Nos.34032, 34005, 34009, and others. *Norman Preedy.*

(above) 9F No.92046 waits its turn at Buttigieg's on 5th July 1968. Its amazing that none of the class figured in the final days of steam working on BR, 'ancient' Stanier Class 5s and 8Fs being preferred to the BR design. This 2-10-0 was a London Midland engine throughout its short life which started at Wellingborough in February 1955 and finished at Birkenhead some twelve years later. Note the timber decking which was useful yard flooring in the absence of concrete. *(below)* In another section of Buttigieg's yard on the same day, ex-LMS 8Fs vie for attention with SR Pacifics. They all got it in the end because there were no escapees from this place! *both Norman Preedy.*

Bird's, Risca:

They obviously liked the BR Standard at the Birds Commercial Motors site at Risca. On show in this summer 1967 image are pieces of Nos.80016, and 80139 whilst in the background No.80133 and sister No.80152 await their fate. Eleven Cl.4 tanks ended up here in total but the yard took care of dozens of other locomotives, mainly ex-Great Western, the most high profile of them being 'King' No.6028; some two-hundred steam locomotives were purchased by the yard. Risca is a town of 11,500 people located within the Caerphilly County Borough in Monmouthshire where Birds set up facilities to handle scrap from various sources in South Wales. In the 1960s the company had a contract to supply scrap metal to the Chinese prior to the 'Cultural Revolution.' Half a dozen Birds scrap yards were dotted about South Wales at the height of the steam scrapping years but they are virtually all gone now as the company diversified into other fields. *Norman Preedy.*

Bird's, Long Marston:

Birds Long Marston yard in Gloucestershire took in a fair number of steam locomotives too, the majority being ex-LMS engines although the GWR was represented by a dozen 'namers' from the Hall, Grange and Manor classes. BR Standard classes consisted of twenty-one engines whilst the ex-LNER contingent comprised eight Thompson B1s. This hulk is 'Jinty No.47272 – you will have to take our word on that – which was one of eight of the class scrapped at Long Marston. On 27th November 1966 it is well on its way to oblivion whilst surrounded by all the detritus expected at a scrapyard; although arguably Birds had this place a mite untidier than most – apparently! This particular yard remained active long after steam had gone and managed to pick off a few BR diesel locomotives thereafter. It is interesting to note the gas cylinders stood about the place like sentinels. The eagle-eyed amongst you will have spotted the single line of railway coming in from the top left of the image; that same piece of track continued to a point beyond the bottom of the illustration. *Norman Preedy.*

Woodham's, Barry:

Early days at the Woodham Bros yard in Barry, or is it? This elevated view of the storage area reveals the inside of the tender of S15 No.30830 which still holds the connecting and coupling rids dumped in there by the fitters who removed them from the 4-6-0s coupled wheels some years previously. Quite a few of the Southern Region Pacifics appear to be without tenders whilst the two North British built A-1-A+A-1-A 'Warships' D600 and D601 are still intact. The first of those to be broken up was D600 in March 1970 so this image obviously predates that event. The accumulation of dirt and vegetation inside the S15's tender shows some years worth of wind and dust so presumably post-dates the end of steam on BR or so it would seem. The actual year is 1967! It appears incredible now and would have perhaps been deemed impossible then but most of the railway mctal in this view has been preserved! *A.R.Thompson coll. (ARPT).*

(above) Another aspect of the Woodham's 'dump' in 1967, from ground level! *(below)* How many times was this 'lowly' goods engine photographed during its tenure at Woodham's. S15 No.30841 with one of those superb double bogie tenders. both *A.R.Thompson coll. (ARPT).*

Crewe Works:

The west end of the vast Scrap shop at Crewe on Sunday 14th June 1964 with a line of Stanier and BR Standard locomotives (minus tenders) waiting for the Monday morning gang to assemble and start the process of breaking them up. Some have already been subject to removal of boiler fitting especially the 8F nearest the camera, No.48010. However, all is not what it seems. *N.W.Skinner (ARPT).*

Same day – 14th June 1964 – same venue; same line-up of locomotives but from the eastern end of the Scrap shop. Stanier Cl.5 No.45425 is nearest the camera now. A group of enthusiasts traipse through the shop en route to the yards and erecting shops. Once again certain boiler fittings have been removed from the engines and, as before, with care. Note also that the every engine had been labelled with its own number stencilled on numerous points of the superstructure. It hardly seems to be the way a condemned locomotive would be treated at this juncture. Finally, in true Crewe fashion, all the engines have arrived in works with their smokebox facing west, courtesy of Crewe South shed turntable. So, what is afoot? From the available evidence neither of the Stanier locomotives mentioned were withdrawn, condemned or anywhere near to being declared 'finished' and of no further use. No.45425 went onto work until the end of 1967 and apparently ended up at a scrapyard in Scotland, 8F No.48010 likewise went through overhaul and worked on towards the end of steam. Seemingly the Scrap Shop was no longer functioning as such and was instead being used to prepare engines for the Erecting Shop, discarding certain worn-out components here before the engines progressed through the works towards the traverser. *N.W.Skinner (ARPT).*

Cowlairs Works:

One of the few Pacifics tackled at Cowlairs was A3 No.60041 SALMON TROUT which was still quite intact in the yard on 30th August 1966. Condemned on 4th December 1965, the engine had provided spares to keep other members of the class in traffic, the cylinders and boiler had gone so far but that appears to be it as the hulk was sold for scrap to Arnott Young in September 1966. What happened to that loose smokebox is unknown but there is every chance that Cowlairs took it off before dispatch to Carmyle. *Norman Preedy.*

Darlington: We have featured Darlington's prodigious feats of breaking up steam locomotives previously in this series. This time however we are mixing the usual 'run-of-the-mill' images with a number of what might be termed 'out-of-the-ordinary' illustrations. It is up to you the reader to make your mind up as to what is what!

Plenty of former LMS locomotives had been cut-up at Darlington before Stanier Cl.3 No.40117 arrived at North Road during the winter of 63/64. This particular engine - which looks to be in a remarkable external condition - was withdrawn from Scarborough shed in November 1962 (it was stored under cover for much of the time prior to dispatch which explains much of what we see) and has ended up at Darlington on 15th February 1964 along with a few more NE Region examples of ex-LMS engines from Copley Hill and Royston sheds. Note the worksplate and numberplate still in situ! *N.W.Skinner (ARPT).*

The Ivatt 2-6-2 tank was classified 2MT by the LMS and looked more 'workmanlike' than the Stanier engine. This is No.41273, ex Farnley Junction shed, in North Road yard on that rather dull 15th February 1964. Push-pull fitted, No.41273 had only been withdrawn during the previous December. The J94 is No.68024. *N.W.Skinner (ARPT).*

Yet another ex-LMS refugee trying to take up residency in the North Road yard on 15th February 1964; Class 4F No.44336 was also condemned in December 1963, and was ex-Normanton. *N.W.Skinner (ARPT).*

A couple of months later and the last of the ex-LMS batch from December 1963 are disappearing. This is Cl.4 No.42407 in April 1964 displayed in a somewhat unique though temporary condition. 1964 was going to be the final complete year of locomotive scrapping activities at North Road. With the nearby locomotive works under sentence too, it was no wonder that BR were bringing in the boundaries around this part of Darlington. *J.W.Armstrong (ARPT).*

Like I mentioned – the unusual! C7 No.2983 awaits its turn on 1st August 1948 but look at the piles of scrap in the foreground. That is correct, WW2 steel helmets amongst the brake shoes and the hose. Most of the helmets appear to be off-white in colour indicating ARP or Civil Defence usage. I suppose it wouldn't be out of place to say that these were ex-LNER helmets that had been collected ready for BR to usher in a new era. Did nobody see the Cold War simmering on the horizon? With hindsight and H&S in mind, BR could have saved thousands of pounds but they weren't in the saving money game were they!? *J.W.Armstrong (ARPT).*

A bleak winter day in 1956 – Sunday 15th January to be exact – with two S1 class eight-coupled hump-shunting tanks being the only occupants (not counting the ghosts) of the yard. Nos.69900 and 69904 are the subject engines and miraculously some twenty-five years separate them. 69900 was one of the original Great Central batch of four from 1907/8 whilst 69904 was built by the LNER in 1932 and had a booster fitted bogie for the first eleven years of its life. Latterly both of these engines were allocated to Doncaster where they did very little work. The coming of large numbers of 350 h.p. diesel-electric shunters in the Fifties' basically took the 0-8-4Ts specialised work away from them and it was difficult to use the half dozen members of the class for anything else. This pair had been withdrawn just nine days beforehand and were the first of the five S1 scrapped at North Road; Doncaster took care of waif No.69903. *J.W.Armstrong (ARPT)*.

During the mid-Fifties' for various reasons, Gorton sent a large number of condemned engines from Manchester to Darlington for cutting up at North Road. Some unusual accounting practices were enacted to transfer the engines including the transfer of active J10s to Darlington shed where upon arrival they were immediately condemned and wheeled into the works for attention! These two ex-GC engines at North Road in May 1956 were withdrawn prior to their journey north and wear the symbols of condemned engines as applied by the works at Gorton. The N5 is No.69340 whilst the J10 is unidentified to us. *J.W.Armstrong (ARPT).*

Two more 'rejects' from Gorton: N5 No.69250 and C13 No.67425 are defiantly still intact at North Road on 27th October 1956 some four weeks after their arrival in the yard. We have illustrated these two at Darlington beforehand albeit not together but this late October Friday image was probably the last recording of the pair before the scrapmen got to work on them during the following week. Note that shed, number and works plates are all still attached! *J.W.Armstrong (ARPT).*

Is it me or does the yard look tidy today? North Road on 4th December 1953 with axles stacked on the right, coal on the left and three intact engines waiting patiently. It appears that the scrapping activity here was somewhat less frantic then. For the record the tender engines were Nos.65023 and 65488. For some reason record of the 0-6-0T has been lost. *J.W.Armstrong (ARPT).*

With two ex-LMS tenders for company, A3 No.60038, or what was left of it, waits at the terminal end of North Road scrapyard on 15th February 1964. The nearest tender has the number 4571 chalked on its flank; this was, it appears, the tender number as it was one of ten straight high-sided 3,500 gallon tenders (numbered 4564 to 4573) built for the 'Jubilee' class engines which were numbered 5607 to 5616. Initially coupled to 'Jubilee' No.5614 LEEWARD ISLANDS, the tender in question had long since been paired with other 'Jubilees' and latterly with 4F 0-6-0s; the engine which brought it to Darlington was No.44604 which was cut up here just days previously alongside J39 No.64818. To reiterate, Darlington certainly dealt with the unusual! *N.W.Skinner (ARPT).*

Here's one of the V2s which didn't get to Swindon. Minus chimney and tender, No.60808 stands waiting amongst the trees with intact WD tenders lurking in the undergrowth – a set of disc wheels from a WD pony truck stands out amongst the rest. Withdrawn on 5th October 1964, the Darlington-built V2 entered works on 15th October 1964 so this image must have been captured soon afterwards with the last vestiges of foliage clinging to the trees. *J.W.Armstrong (ARPT).*

It may be some fourteen years too soon to qualify for inclusion in this series but this illustration of Raven A2 No.2402 CITY OF YORK is worth the flak from the Publisher which might hit the editorial team Virtually intact, the Pacific awaits its fate inside the North Road yard at the end of August 1936. Note that the nameplate is still in situ, a practice which carried on into BR days when most of the D49s cut up here in 1961 entered the yard with nameplates, and everything else, attached; it is still wonderment to this writer that none of those plates went missing overnight, or did they? Although not the best looking of the LNER Pacifics, the Raven A2 still exuded the massive power which that boiler was capable of producing or may have done if the firebox had been larger. The yard here was not as busy in those pre-war days and I'm sure that the scrapping gang was nowhere near as big as that which greeted withdrawn locomotives during the last decade of operations here. *J.W.Armstrong coll., (ARPT).*

Sister No.2404 the former CITY OF RIPON in 1937. The boiler – No.7791 – had been taken off on 17th March and sent to Doncaster because it was one of the Gresley A1 boilers which had been fitted to the engine in 1929; the only one carried by the Raven engines. Note the profile of the boiler cut-out in the cab which had been adapted and enlarged to accept the larger firebox of the Gresley boiler. Condemned in February, this remaining portion of the engine was cut up in June 1937. *J.W.Armstrong coll., (ARPT).*

Wounded and not quite out of its misery, J39 No.64925 is being slowly cut to pieces on 29th March 1963. Note the numberplate still attached to the smokebox door; it was often the case that the doors were removed with the plate in situ, the job of removing the plate being left for someone else. The year 1962 – not to mention 60' and 61' – proved to be devastating for J39 class, their elimination being completed by BR workshops. Darlington's contribution to their demise was rather small in comparison to other works and our subject here was one of the last examples dealt with at North Road; a sister resides on the other side of the yard. *N.W.Skinner* (ARPT).

(above) A line-up from 22nd October 1960 containing the usual suspects found loitering in these parts: Nos.68072, 61440, 65777, 68269, 68316, and 68410. *David J.Dippie. (below)* A pair of ex-North Eastern Atlantics – C7s Nos.62982 and 62988, both built in 1915 and both condemned on 24th July 1948 – became BR scrapping candidates and grace the yard on 15th October 1948. *J.W.Armstrong (ARPT).*

Electric locomotive No.26504 still carries the North Eastern markings nearly thirty years after that Company became history. It still has the No.5 cast number plate on the end panels – those plates were 24 inches wide – but the BR number 26504 gives away the fact that this image was captured in late 1950. No.5 was the only one of the ten-strong class to survive in the NER livery, a situation aided by the fact that the engine had spent most of the LNER period in store at Shildon, Darlington and latterly Gosforth. It was scrapped at Darlington so that its twin bogies could be salvaged as spares for sister 26510, later to become Departmental 100 based at Ilford! No.26504 was the only one of the class cut up at Darlington; one succumbed at Doncaster in 1964 (DM 100), whilst the other eight went to a private yard near Sheffield during 1950 – a taster of things to come!? *J.W.Armstrong* (ARPT).

Keeping up the 'modern image' trend, we present this view of J67 No.68559 – ex-Gorton – and 350 h.p. diesel-electric shunter 13227. Although undated, we can approximate the image to circa late May 1956. The diesel was Darlington built from December 1955 but it was sent initially to Newport on the Tees but transferred to Darlington 51A six weeks later. It was renumbered D3227 in April 1962 at Darlington. Withdrawn at Gateshead in November 1985 as 08159, the 0-6-0DE was cut-up at Doncaster in the summer of 1986. So, that narrows the date down to anywhere from late January 1956 to March 1962. However, the 0-6-0T became a temporary resident of North Road yard after its arrival from Wrexham via Gorton in late May 1956 (it was sent to Darlington from Gorton on 16th May). This could therefore, as already stated, be late May 1956. The rarity value of this illustration is not the J67 but the diesel of which few images exist of their presence in the scrapyard, albeit delivering thirty-odd tons of scrap metal. One final question! Note the foliage on the tree in the left background; does that indicate the start of summer or were the trees around North Road dying? *J.W.Armstrong (ARPT).*

47

No going back! The boiler and smokebox of Thompson B1 No.61242 grounded at North Road yard on 21st November 1964. Note the nameplate still attached. Such 'trivia' was not a worry for the scrapmen. Their job was to dismantle locomotives and get the resultant smaller pieces into the 16-ton mineral wagons ready for despatch. There might also have been an element of piece-work involved, in which case the nameplate was lucky to survive thus far. *N.W.Skinner (ARPT).*

We couldn't do Darlington without an image of a WD 2-8-0, no matter how painful. This is No.90663 in May 1964. The screen of trees had certainly come on over recent years, and they managed to mask some of the yard activity and noise from the outside world. The location could in fact be anywhere but it was North Road, I think!?! *J.W.Armstrong (ARPT).*

In this undated view of the yard, a group of visiting enthusiasts decided to use the place, unwittingly of course, as an assault course. The image is a reminder of how dangerous such an establishment could be but did you ever hear of any injuries or fatalities? The line of withdrawn A8s tell us that diesel multiple units had successfully taken over most of the stopping passenger services in the region. *K.Linford (ARPT)*.

(opposite) From my first visit of North Road yard I always linked the place to the surreal, mysterious and strange. The fact that you could virtually walk into the yard at weekends without the usual ritual of trying to prove that you were not up to anything illegal, etc. It certainly was different from any other scrapyard I visited. This image is typical of what I am trying to explain – a water fountain, complete with ornamental masonry, slap bang on the edge of the yard located on the boundary of industrial and residential Darlington. *J.W.Armstrong (ARPT)*.

A most unusual view of the scrapyard with only one locomotive present – a 'Jinty' apparently – whilst wagons of varying types fill the sidings. It is unclear, though perhaps obvious to some, which were for scrapping and which ones were there to take away the scrap. The two steam cranes will no doubt earn their keep over the following days. It seems that normal practice was to scrap as many locomotives as possible using the available space to the maximum. Once the spaces were filled with scrap, wagons were shunted into the yard and a clean-up lasting up to a week would take place thereafter. Very tidy housekeeping, which ever way you look at it. Then, the next lot would be wheeled in and cutting up would resume – a veritable production line! *Maurice Burns.*

An identical view to that shown opposite which was captured in 1959 with numerous locomotives waiting their turn, amongst them D49 No.62730 (11th December 1958) and J25 No.65655 (2nd December 1958); withdrawn some months beforehand on the dates indicated. *Maurice Burns.*

Two views of the North Road scrapyard at Darlington after the 'cessation of hostilities' and with the clear-up nearly complete. Not every locomotive cut-up at Darlington passed through this yard, the works also took care of some of them, but the numbers which entered this place was in the hundreds and for variety was probably second to none. The range of buildings on show constituted some of the oldest railway premises in Britain – so what happened to them? both *Maurice Burns.*

Derby Works:

This Shoeburyness based 3-cylinder Class 4, No.42512, was the first of the class to be withdrawn, a deed that was carried out in November 1960. Here in the works at Derby on 13th November 1960, the 2-6-4T looks decidedly unwell having already lost its boiler. The whole class of these London–Tilbury based tanks was maintained by Derby after being built there but surprisingly only six were actually broken up there. Doncaster took care of the bulk of the class with no less than twenty-six entering the 'Plant Works' for attention; Crewe apparently saw off three of their number whilst Stratford took care of one. The class leader was preserved! Six months would pass before another of the class, No.42507, was condemned. *N.W.Skinner (ARPT).*

Six months later, at the same location on 7th May 1961 and Fowler Cl.4 No.42337 appears to be in dire straits but the 2-6-4T was simply being stripped and made ready for shops. It would be another two years and a half years before the Birmingham based 4P was withdrawn. *N.W.Skinner (ARPT).*

Another Fowler tank waits for the chop at Derby on 7th April 1963. Class 3 No.40022 was one of the apparently less successful 'Breadvans', smaller versions of the versatile and highly regarded Class 4. This example was condenser-fitted and worked from either Cricklewood or Kentish Town sheds on employment which took them over the Metropolitan lines, hence the condenser apparatus. No.40022 was withdrawn at Cricklewood shed in December 1962 and had just reached Derby. *N.W.Skinner (ARPT).*

Doncaster Works:

On the road to oblivion! A4 No.60014 SILVER LINK in the yard at Doncaster on the 5th May 1963 with one of the 3-cylinder Stanier Cl.4 tanks from the Tilbury line, and a former LNER built 350 h.p. diesel-electric shunter. If any A4 was deserved of preservation it was No.14 – the first of the class – but BR had other ideas with No.22, admittedly another deserving engine, getting the stamp of approval. The unidentified 2-6-4T was of course Eastern Region property through boundary changes implemented by BR from the earliest days of the creation of the national concern when all the London, Tilbury & Southend line was taken over by the ER. Derby looked after the maintenance of the locomotives but when scrapping of the class became necessary Derby exercised its options not to entertain ER based locomotives any more; hence the fact that most of the class were broken up at Doncaster. The diesel shunter was not one of the four ex-LNER J45s based at March but was the singleton which was late in being taken into BR stock having been completed by the LNER just prior to Nationalisation. Numbered 15004, the 0-6-0DE was allocated latterly to New England depot and was and condemned in October 1962. It too was cut up at Doncaster in May 1963, probably the first diesel locomotive scrapped there. This temporary little gathering therefore was somewhat special in the great scheme! *George Watson (ARPT).*

Not strictly a scene from the scrapyard or an image of condemned locomotives. However, it is worth including this illustration inside the works on 24th April 1949 when two of the C1 Atlantics were being used as Stationary Boilers (SBs). As can be seen, the Heath Robinson style conglomeration looked quite permanent but of course it was far from it. For the record, the two engines were Nos.3274 and 3285, both of which met their eventual ends at Doncaster. *K.H.Cockerill (ARPT).*

Two adjacent K3s, No.61941 and 61920, are the subject of this image which was captured on 20th August 1961. The pair were seemingly in near-identical states, although one retains its connecting and coupling rods, for now. A month had passed since someone had emptied the tender tank and left the chalkcd message that it had been attended to on 21st July. This shows the haste with which some locomotives were broken up, Doncaster being rather good at scrapping locomotives before they were reported as condemned never mind broken up. *N.W.Skinner (ARPT).*

Another cabless hulk. This is V2 No.60867 on the 5th May 1962. Even without its cab and smokebox the 2-6-2 looks to be a match for almost anything.
N.W.Skinner (ARPT).

Derby was sending steam locomotives to Doncaster for cutting up long before the LT&S Cl.4s were withdrawn in any numbers. This scene of Doncaster's scrapyard was captured on 8th May 1960 and features two of the LMS-built 4P Compounds dispatched from Derby that year, Nos.41090 and 41102. Although from the same Derby-built batch and lot, the two engines have a number of visible detail differences, the dome covers for instance, the positioning of either outside or inside steam pipes; livery, and other details. Derby, it will be noted, has removed the works and number plates but the 4-4-0s had already been withdrawn for eighteen months prior to Doncaster receiving them. *N.W.Skinner (ARPT).*

Remember No.5 at Darlington in 1950. Sister No.26510 was mentioned and here she is at Doncaster in 1964 having outlived her siblings by fourteen years or so. Looking quite neglected, the Bo-Bo had done little in the way of haulage its pantographs having been removed at some unknown date. Looking at the large sandboxes arranged around the bogies, it must have taken some time to prepare this engine and its sisters for any work. *I.Spencer.*

Hardy souls look amongst the remains in the desolate winter landscape of the scrapyard at Doncaster before the modernisation. The date is 9th March 1958, a Sunday. Identifiable were parts and pieces of Nos.68882, 69558, 67362, and 69597. Many of those gentlemen in the picture are hopefully still with us although they are now getting on in years. *W.R.E.Lewis (ARPT).*

Swindon Works:

Swindon Stock Shed yard circa 1959, with a number of locomotives lying idle either through retirement, or temporary storage. Those identifiable include various six-coupled engines which never left the place again and were broken up in 1960 or 1961: Nos.1616, 2266, 2296 and 6725. The fascination of visiting main works always included locations such as this where locomotives could be stored for years. Latterly though the throughput of even the storage areas would get hectic as engines were either sold for scrap or quickly dealt with at the works. Although Swindon had the scrapping shed known as 'C' Shop, it was soon realised that that particular facility could not handle the required throughput of condemned locomotives if backlogs in the scrapping process were to be avoided. *Norman Preedy.*

Amongst the last of the steam locomotives scrapped at Swindon was 1400 Class 0-4-2T No.1451 which is seen going through the process during a
66 break on Sunday 26th July 1964. Deceptively, some forty tons of various metals were involved here. *Norman Preedy.*

During the great cull of the 'Kings' in 1962, it was possible to catch many of them at Swindon although most were taken care of by private yards – Cox & Danks scrapped eleven of them – with Swindon only managing ten! One of the latter batch was No.6008 KING JAMES II which was photographed intact – except for its Stafford Road shedplate – on 12th August 1962, shortly after its arrival at the works from Wolverhampton. Withdrawn on the previous 19th June, the 4-6-0 was to languish at the works for nearly a year prior to cutting up. *Norman Preedy.*

One 'King' which did make it to 'C' Shop was No.6004 KING GEORGE III. Withdrawn on 19th September 1962, this is all that remained of the engine on the following 21st October, a Sunday, with enthusiasts milling around the wheeled frames. It was finally destroyed during the week ending Saturday 3rd November. Note that the wagons employed are all wooden-bodied opens with not a 16-ton steel mineral wagon in sight. *Norman Preedy.*

Unmistakably Swindon but the identity of the 'Castle' is not so certain although someone has chalked 5069 on the cabside. The date has also been lost but No.5069 was one of the class which did succumb at Swindon, the former Laira engine being condemned in February 1962 and apparently cut up during the following May. This particular 'Castle' carried the name ISAMBARD KINGDOM BRUNEL, a moniker which you would have thought may have perhaps secured a more positive future for 5069. But it was not to be; the BTC held the keys to what was officially preserved and enthusiasts were still toying with the fact that the little engines might be viable risks for private preservation. Big engines were certainly not yet seen as feasible by private parties, but times were about to change. *Norman Preedy.*

Still wearing the old BR emblem, but with its numberplate removed, No.4585 awaits its lot at Swindon on 7th February 1960. Another six-coupled sister, the larger but now tender-less No.5393, completes the picture of despair on an otherwise glorious Sunday afternoon. *C.J.B.Sanderson (ARPT).*

It was inevitable that an outside working area would be created at Swindon to dismantle the numerous condemned engines dealt with by the works during those heady days of the early 1960s; a time when the Region was trying its hardest – and succeeding – to get rid of steam motive power. This was the yard on 23rd June 1963 with a selection of ten locomotives, mainly tender engines headed up by an unidentified 'Prairie' which was about to be broken up. F.W.Hampson (ARPT).

Two 'Panniers' grace the scrap yard on different dates: No.3711 *(above)* on the morning of Sunday 23rd June 1963, and condenser-fitted No.9702 *(below)* on the previous 9th September 1962 – another Sunday. No.9702 was built at Swindon in September 1933 and was fitted from the start with the condensing apparatus for working certain lines in the London area. Like the other ten members of this small sub-class, she was allocated to Old Oak Common depot. Withdrawn in May 62' she was scrapped later in the year. No.3711 was in fact the younger of the pair and was put into traffic in November 1936. In 1958 the 0-6-0PT was converted to oil-burning by Robert Stephenson & Hawthorn (Newcastle) but for how long is unknown. Withdrawn in May 1963, she was broken up in November. *both F.W.Hampson (ARPT).*

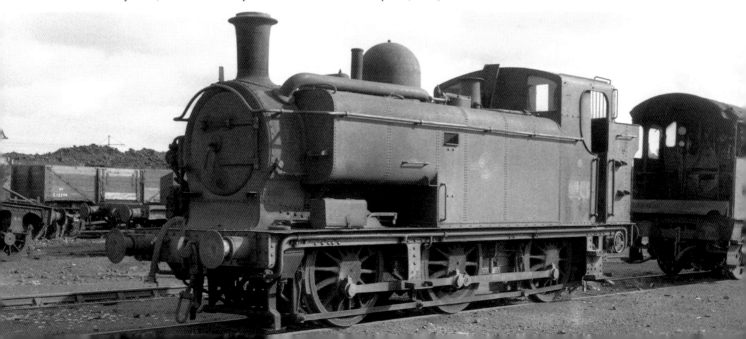